"Let's go Buford, hurry! The water is coming in too fast" I frantically appealed. "I have to go back and get George Brett" he demanded. No, its not a person or a cat if that's what you're thinking, it's a baseball card. "You're going to drown you dummy" I yelled. The wind was howling outside the fort and the rain was pounding the roof. "I'm going in" as he held his breath and disappeared through the hole in the wall, muddy water gushing all around him like he'd just jumped into a big bowl of chocolate pudding. It's dark and I'm looking in but can't see anything, "dang it!" I hear in a gobbly screach. "He's not in here!" By now the hole is completely submerged in water and all I can hear is splashing. I started moving our sleeping bags and boxes of baseball and football cards to higher ground. The light from my flashlight is beaming a serious gleam at the hole that my best friend just disappeared through. Finally, a wet bristly head pops through the flooded hole. "Puuuff" as he lets out air from holding his breath. "I didn't find him, he must have been swept away" he said. The water was starting to invade our space. We dragged our damp sleeping bags up the ladder to the lookout. We looked at each other through the beam of the flashlight in disbelief. "well, I guess your dad was right!"(earlier in the night my Dad said we were going to have to swim out of here), Buford said. "We'll have to sleep up here tonight, we're not getting out of here until the rain stops," he added. That being said, let's see how we got to that moment shall we.

Chapter 1

RUN OF TOWN

I'm Johnny and this is my story of the fort, it was 1982, I was your typical 11 year old kid, at least I thought so. I was rather skinny and tan, I had straight brown hair that I combed straight down. My "go to" outfit was a pair of sport shorts and a tee shirt. With my white high-top shoes, I wore white socks with a blue, green or red band around the top and pulled them up to my knees.

I liked to pogo stick, walk on stilts, fish, play football, collect baseball cards and matchbooks and mow lawns. I was a master at my handheld electronic football game and I could solve the Rubiks cube. Ms. Pacman and Galaga were the coolest video games in all the arcades. We could play them for hours with the money we earned from mowing lawns, I'd typically earn $7 per lawn or we'd get quick cash by just going around town and picking up cans and earn $.05 for each one found. It only took 5 cans to get a candy bar. Back then if you had a dollar you could get a Milky Way for a quarter along with a glass bottle of pop for a quarter and still have enough for 2 games. Once we got a little older we could put one quarter in a pinball machine and play for hours. The machine would make a loud "knock" every time we won a game.

We had the run of the whole town. It was a small town with a town square and a lot of places for a kid like me to go. No place was out of reach, you could get all the way across town within 10 minutes. Anywhere your bike could take you. I didn't ride my bike though, I drove it. The sidewalks were my highway and the more bumps and contours the better. I'd cruise down the shaded sidewalks, dodging the low hanging branches and an occasional old lady walking along, high fiving the drooping maple leaves as I coasted by. The best sidewalks to drive on were the old brick sidewalks, you'd think they'd be bumpy, but it felt like you're riding on a smoothed-out dirt trail with occasional dips and mounds. I had a Honda mini bike and I liked to ride that too, but I was limited to where I could go. Pretty much just in a circle around the back yard and as I'd rip through the gears and hit 30-35 mph, the thrill was soon gone because I'd run out of trail. My 12-speed gave me freedom.

I usually went to the pool or down to the creek or to the golf course for a quick 9 holes. Going uptown was the best though. You could go to the fountain shop (they made the best cherry cokes), the general store or the gas station where in the back they had the latest video games and racks of candy bars. Thumbing through record albums at the general store was a weekly affair, Michael Jackson's Thriller was out that year and I picked that up as soon as I had $8.99 to spare.

You see, it was a lot different than now-a- days. We didn't have computers. Cable TV was kind of new and scarce in most areas. We did have satellite tv though, the dish was the size of a small car, it would slowly turn as you changed channels. The Atari 2600, which was the first home gaming system available, was cool for us but it didn't keep us from going out into the big world outside. The video games didn't have addictive qualities and the graphics were ancient compared to the games of the 2000's. You wouldn't sit and play "Tanks" all day which is basically, a square, with a stick poking out of it shooting dots at another tank while there's a continuous rumble coming through the tv speaker and a ping sound when you fire. Not too exciting.

Chapter 2

SCHOOLS OUT

The summer of that year was upon us, just minutes away, we were about to bust out of school and we were going out in style this year. Next year we had to merge in with the high schoolers at a different building so no more "big man on campus" attitude, we were going to the bottom of the food chain. It's a little scary going to another building, a different principal and a bunch of older kids that you tried to stay away from when they were in grade school. I wasn't really looking forward to it because I heard you get a lot of homework in 7th grade but I wasn't going to worry about that right now. A cool kid named Stewpot brought his boombox that day and at 3:20, he pushed play, and "schools out for the summer" blared out of the speakers sucking every bit of juice from those 8 "D" batteries that powered it.

The teacher in the hall tried to keep us quiet, it was no use, we did not care at that point, we could see the light shining through the double doors outside to the playground. We strutted down that warm musty hallway with the distorted music washing out the sounds from the slamming of locker after locker, we were free! No idea what the summer had in store for me, I didn't have any plans, no job, no summer school, I didn't have a girlfriend, well I kind of did, it was Olivia Newton John, she was a famous singer and I carved JP + ONJ in a tree to proclaim my love. It was a one-sided love, I had a crush on her but she obviously had no idea who I was. Her song "Physical" was at the top of the charts and she was my girl and I didn't worry about the other girls, they were all taller than me anyway. Plus, girls weren't cool, farts and baseball cards were cool. I was going to spend my summer doing only fun stuff. I hopped on my bike, "schools out for the summer, schools out forever!" I sang, book bag swaying on my handle bars with every peddle and rode off into the summer I'd never forget.

I got home that afternoon and through the door I could smell it, a horrific smell. Canned beets! My mom was always in the kitchen, 99.99% of the time it was wonderful, you always had a second helping at dinner, but when it was beet season and she'd been out picking in the garden, look out! I don't know who eats something that stinks so bad but I sure didn't. As I waited for supper, I called Buford, 3817, that's all you had to dial on the phone. His mom answered, "Hellooooo" in a Julia Childs style voice, "Is Buford home?" I asked. "Not right now, he's walking his dog Fudge" she said, "Oh, wait a minute he just came in," "uh hello?" he said, "It's Johnny, what are you doing tomorrow?" "I don't know" he said. "Let's go get some donuts in the morning and go down to the creek and do some fishing," I said, "Sounds good," he replied. We spent that next day catching chubs and screwing around down at the creek. We were going to have some fun for these next 87 days, I could tell.

Chapter 3

BEST BUDS

You'll have a lot of different friends as you up. At some point one or two of them will be considered your best friends. I was lucky, I found a couple of my best friends years before in 2nd grade. In the middle school years, you shake out who's in your circle of friends. Everyone is friends in elementary but in 6th grade you start to get your gang together and if you're lucky they'll be with you through high school and beyond. That's when my buddy Buford and I started hanging around together more.

We were all pretty much nerds at that point but if there was anyone that was considered cool it was him. Except for the time when he wore the same shirt for school pictures 2 years in a row, not very cool. Every recess pretty much all the boys in the class would play football, every day, even in the winter. If I got on Buford's team, we had an advantage. We had our own playbook. He was the quarterback always and I was just good enough to be a receiver. We'd mastered the plays in my backyard after school and he'd shout out a name and I'd run the route. "Shotgun Grasspicker" or "Beebus" he'd yell. No one knew what the heck was going on, we were ahead of the game. In high school we'd go on to win a state championship in football.

Chapter 4

DOWN TO BUSINESS

During the prior school year, Buford had been building a fort with his buddy Bobby. It was a big wood box with carpet stuck all over the inside and a little hole to wiggle through to get in. I'd been in it and the only way you could see anything was to have a candle going inside. It smelled like Cheetos and sour milk. Oh, also it had newspaper for insulation. Talking about a fire hazard, what a couple of morons. Well as you've probably guessed, that baby went up in flames! Luckily no one was hurt in the fort fire, but it did present an opportunity. It was Bobby's bright idea to have a candle that engulfed the place, so it wasn't to hard to sway Buford into forming a new partnership and I had the perfect spot for a fort.

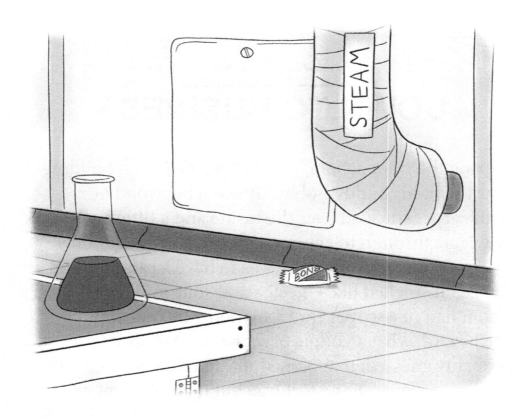

We'd already had a year-long secret operation of hiding
candy in the wall in our science class. We found a hole
by the steam pipe where we fabricated a piece to look
exactly like the wall and slid it over the hole. We'd get
there first thing in the morning before the teacher came
in and took our stash out of our bookbags and hid it
in there. That way we could go back during reading
time, slide off the cover from the secret hole and chow
down on sprees and 'Now and Laters' while we looked
for pictures of boobies in the National Geographic
magazines, so we were already in business together to
some degree.

Chapter 5
THE BUILD BEGINS

To get our new fort going we took some of the scorched
wood from Bobby and Buford's fort to our new site. We
had to haul it about a mile from his house, but it got us
started. "We're gonna need some more wood" I said.
There were some houses being built near our site so we
started hauling what we could on our bikes to our site.
The amount of wood and materials we transported on
our bikes that summer would easily fill the back of 2
pickup trucks. We never asked our parents for help and
they never bothered us, we just did what we had to do
no matter how crazy it looked. "We can get some nails
from my garage" said Buford. "I don't think my dad will
notice if some are gone" Our site was set in a ditch in a
line of trees, just off the street with a field in back. We
had no plans just a couple of hammers, a shovel and an
old rusty handsaw and we just started building.

"Let's dig a basement" I said.

The basement of the first room would take the form of a small 2 person hot tub with a deep middle and sides all around that we called the couch. Then we dug the tornado room which ended up being about 2 feet below that.

The tornado room was like a basement and it was between 2 trees. We left holes in the walls to allow wind to blow through. We were able to score some big sheets of lumber from nearby that we used for the roof on the main room. Without any plans, we just started nailing wood together. The structure started to take shape, we were constantly running out of nails though and didn't want to waste our candy money by buying them at the hardware store. Buford's dad had to wonder what was happening to his supply, we took a pocketful of nails from his garage every time we were there. We'd also have to stop by his kitchen since his mom always had something good that she had baked. On school field trips, he'd always have the best brownies or cookies, that kid could eat sugar like no other.

Chapter 6

TAKING SHAPE

We always had music going, we had the radio dial set to the pop station. Our theme song was "I Ran" by A Flock of Seagulls. Every time that came on we'd crank it up and work harder. "I ran, I ran so far awaaayy" we'd sing. The other song that got us fired up was "Trouble" by Lindsey Buckingham. The sound floated out through the neighborhood, our voices trying hard to harmonize along the way. Well at least I was, Buford couldn't sing a note, it sounded a lot like loud mumbles or a sick toad. As the construction continued, we just kind of built it based on the size of the pieces of wood we had. It had walls and an arched roof like a regular house. "I don't know Buford, we need to put something on the roof to keep it from leaking." I stated. "The only thing I can think of is plastic bags or something like that" he said. The fort was turning out nicer than we had thought.

It ended up having multiple rooms all with their own character. We wanted to put carpet in the place, so we needed to waterproof the roof. "Let's go uptown and go dumpster diving", said Buford. We took off. We knew where a lot of big dumpsters were behind businesses uptown since we'd always check them for cans. Once we got to the furniture store we hit the jackpot. "Holy crap, A waterbed! This is awesome!" I exclaimed. I knew what one of those looked like since I had one for my bed. The one in the dumpster must have popped but it was a huge rubbery sheet we could use to cover our whole roof. I grabbed one end and Buford grabbed the other and we carted the dripping bladder home between us on our bikes. "Let's get this baby back and see if it fits" I said. "Hey, maybe we should stop over at the donut shop and get a couple of donuts" Buford said. "No, my mom has some scotcharoos at home, we'll get one of those" I said. "You're always hungry!"

A lot of the materials we found were used. We spent
a lot of time pulling nails out of boards and then
pounding them straight. "Gonna pull some nails"
we'd say. The nails never came out perfectly straight,
but you get to be pretty good at nailing when you're
pounding a slightly curved nail. Another never ending
job was patching. We had such a variety of wood sizes
and shapes that putting them together to form walls
inevitably left small cracks or gaps so we'd patch them
and stuff newspaper in the cracks. A trick Buford
must've learned from Bobby. Even though we weren't
getting paid, it was a job to us, one we enjoyed. We'd
show up in the morning and work. We would go
uptown to the soda fountain for lunch, a tuna sandwich
for $1.15 and a homemade cherry coke or my mom
would make us something. The fort was taking shape
and we were starting to just go down and hang out.
Little did we know word was spreading about our fort
and people were getting curious as to what was going
on.

Once we were finished the fort ended up having an entry way that looked like an A-Frame. To get in you'd lift up a 4 foot by 4 foot door. This was our first line of defense because we could lock it from inside and the only way through it would be to blow it up or saw through it. Then you'd be to the main door of the living room, which also had a lock on it. You go through there and into our living room which was "L" shaped with a ledge made from the dirt all around that acted as our couch. We had orange colored carpet that hugged the contour of the ground we'd dug out. We had some posters in there, a picture of Olivia and Cheryl Tiegs along with a shelf where we stored all our stuff.

Above that room was a secret room with a hidden opening in the ceiling of the living room. We never went up there, it was too hot like an attic, but in case we needed to hide nobody would find us there. There was a side room off the living room that we called the wind room. Off the back was the tornado room. You could stand up in this room, the rest of the rooms you had to be on your knees. We needed power down there and since my garage wasn't too far away we patched together all my dad's extension cords and ran a plug into the fort. We had a lamp and then could plug in the radio, that's all we needed. We'd have to roll up the cord when we left since we strung it across the road, but it was better than using candles for light! No fire in our fort!

Chapter 7

SLEEPLESS NIGHT

One night we were hanging out and it was real late, around 1:00 a.m. All of sudden we heard a car pull up. We could here muffled sounds and little beams of light from the headlights were shining through some of the cracks in our walls where we missed patching. "Shut off the music," I whispered. "who is it?" I asked. "I don't know," Buford responded. We didn't move a muscle; our bikes were up at my house so there wasn't anything outside that would indicate we were there. We could hear our hearts beating in the quiet, our doors were locked tight and we just sat there. "If they try to break in, let's sneak up to the secret room," Buford whispered. We could here them walking around, they were trying to find an opening to get in. We waited and listened, then car doors closed. The sound of the car disappeared. We don't know who it was or what they wanted but they didn't get in. We didn't sleep very well that night.

Chapter 8

BUILT TO LAST

One afternoon, a terrible storm was a brewing and we were excited to see if the fort would hold up. As the rain came down we sat patiently, "no leaks!" we exclaimed. We were thrilled, the waterbed kept all the rain out. We jumped down into the tornado room and wind was blowing through the vents, just as designed. All of a sudden, "CRACK!" the sound sent shivers up and down our spines. "Holy crap", Buford yelled. A tree had fallen within inches of the fort and it looked like it'd been hit by lightning. "That was the biggest boom I've ever heard!" he added. All in all, everything was just fine and the storm passed. We pulled the tree away and were proud the fort had withstood a wicked test.

Chapter 9

GIRLS, GIRLS, GIRLS

"Let's meet at the gas station and play some video games first" I said. "Ok" he agreed. "I heard Stewpot got the high score on Ms. Pacman" I said. We rode up to the gas station and could only get to the pretzel stage of Ms. Pacman, "STU" was still the high score at the top. At the movie theatre I grabbed a bag of Twizzlers and Coke. Buford got a box of chocolate covered raisins and we found our seat. Not before too long, someone had their pink Ked's shoes on the back of our chairs, kicking every now and then. It was a bunch of girls from our grade. Not only were they taller than us but they were also much more mature. We didn't want to talk to them but here we are right in their eyesight. We just wanted to watch the movie. A piece of popcorn flew up and hit Buford right in the ear, "hey, knock it off!" he coughed choking on one of his raisins. "oh you big baby" they said. He chucked a couple raisins back at them. We watched the movie but felt like we were being watched the whole time. The movie was a little sad at one part and I had a tear in my eye which I quickly brushed away so the girls wouldn't see me crying. A chocolate covered raisin that Buford had tossed back at the girls ended up on the seat of one of them that was wearing yellow shorts. She must have sat on it for the entire movie. As we left the theatre, there was a big smushy brown spot on the back of the girl's shorts, we had to laugh about that. "See you tomorrow," we told each other high fiving as we left.

After the movie I jumped on my bike and headed home, I had to hurry because I had to pee. I started off, "oooh" I thought to myself, "it's a lot cooler than it was before the movie". I rode past the court house square and down the tree lined streets of where my house was. "I've never had to pee this bad in my life!" "I gotta stop" I thought but where? I certainly wasn't going to make it home and in the distance of 2 blocks I had made the decision, I'm going to pee off the side of my bike while I go down the big hill to my house. I had shorts on and they were stretchy. At the top of the hill I let it out, what a relief. I was moving along pretty fast by now and coming out of the trees to where the street lights were lighting up the bottom of the hill. I can't stop peeing now, I'll pee all over myself and if someone is outside walking along the sidewalk they're going to see me, luckily no one was out. The faster I went though the harder it was to keep it from splashing on my bike. I cruised past the baseball diamond and finished up. I was soon walking through my front door, "How was the movie?" mom asked. "It was really good!" I said with a smile.

Chapter 10

BOYS ONLY

We spent a lot of time in the fort, especially when it was hot, it was always nice and cool in our basement. The mice from the field had been enjoying the place also. There were a lot of mice running around with rotten teeth because they got up on our candy shelf and helped themselves one night. Just a bunch of little bites and paper shreds all over. We solved that problem with a glass jar and a lid.

"I'll trade you George Brett for those 3 guys and your blue elephant eraser you call beebus" I said, "deal!" yelled Buford smiling with what must have been a whole pack of "Now and Laters" in his mouth. That was the best thing about having your own place to go. You could say the stupidest things without any adult telling you to watch your mouth. You could eat all the junk food that you wanted to and nobody could stop you. It was our own little world.

We were just sitting there trading cards, eating candy and we heard giggling outside. "Who's that?" Buford whispered, we looked out our peek hole and how could it be? "They found us!" It was a couple of girls from the movie. These girls are starting to be a pain in our butts. It was a few months earlier and the fast running long legged girls of the grade ran us down on May Day and smacked a kiss right on our lips after we dropped off May Day baskets (which we'd eaten all the candy out of leaving just dry popcorn) on their doorstep. I should say on my lips because Buford got away and just watched from down the block and laughed as they terrorized me with tickles on my stomach and kisses all over my face.

"Just be quiet, maybe they won't know we're in here"
I said. "No dummy, they can see our bikes right out
front." he said. "Can we come in?" Holly asked, "uh no"
we replied. A lot of silence and some more giggling
and we just sat there. "Why don't you guys come out?"
she asked. "no, we're busy" we said. Now years later
we'd both be chasing this very girl and here we are
denying her entrance into our fort. We decided early
on that if someone wanted in they had to buy in with
either money for candy or nails and wood, this was no
exception. We did feel a little sorry for them I guess
but they weren't going to be allowed in this boy's club, it
was boy's only and it was ok back then. We did decide
that we'd build them a fort next to ours. "Come back
tomorrow and we'll build you a fort" we said. That
fort took about 10 minutes to build. It was 4 pieces of
plywood, it had 3 sides and a roof.

You could get one person in it, it was like getting into a sleeping bag. We could barely hit the head of the nails we were laughing so hard building it. The next day, here they come, all excited to see their fort and they weren't very happy but we were still laughing. After they saw that, they must have got the hint because we didn't see them down there for the rest of the summer.

We had others try to join our fort club, but they never hung around for more than a day. I think it was partly because we usually tinkered around and worked on things, it wasn't for everyone. We had one kid bribe us with a Playboy magazine he stole from his dad. We kept it for a while, but the kid didn't come back and having that naked girl magazine around made us nervous. We ended up sneaking it down to the creek and burying it in the bank. I stumbled across it when I had a trapping line as a teenager. It was very close to a raccoon trap I had set. It had been exposed by rain and the current from the creek. The pages were frozen and essentially preserved. I cracked it open for a second and chucked it out into the icy water.

Chapter 11

SUMMER FUN

We'd been filling our days with so much work we kind of forgot about the rest of the fun stuff to do during summer. It was time to take a break. "Let's go to the pool, I'm going to do a can opener off the high board and splash the life guards!" I said. "Yeah, I bet you can't" Buford said. Off we went on our bikes racing through the hot summer air, just shoes on and our swim-trunks with our towels wrapped around our shoulders. We walked right over to the high board and got in line. I got myself ready, that high board must have been 20 feet high and super bouncy so you could really get a good jump. I took off and soared through the air angled at the life guard stand, splash! "Johnny!" she yelled and blew her whistle but winked at me as I got out. "Watch out!" she said. The lifeguards at the pool loved us, at least in our minds they did. We were way too young to be any threat to their boyfriends, so we got away with teasing them. We thought it was flirting, I'm certain they thought it was annoying. "Hi Johnny" they'd say in a chorus with a melodic sound. Who needs a girlfriend when the hottest girls in town sing your name when you come walking through the pool gates.

"Abra abracadabra, I want to reach out and grab ya" played over the pool speakers. I couldn't be happier, floating around, soaking up the sun with no sunscreen on when all of a sudden, I go down. I'm dunked from behind and it doesn't feel like Buford. I've been tackled by him, this was someone softer with what felt like greasy skin. I'm flailing around, water up my nose and I break free, turn around shaking off my head and its Holly and her posse', Buford is out of sight doing cannonballs off the diving board and doesn't see me in a battle. "What are you doing?!" I quizzed. "Just havin fun" she said splashing me in the face. I can still hear the Abracadabra song playing, I looked around and back at Buford, I didn't want him to see me talking to the girls. I leaped out of the water and on to her shoulders and she went under. By this time, Buford saw what was going on and jumped in for backup. A lot of laughing was going on and at that moment, I started to realize something. "you know what", I said to myself, "these girls aren't that bad"

Could it be? I never thought about hanging out with girls before but now I'm thinking that I kind of like it. We splashed around until the "everyone out call" came over the loudspeaker. I jumped out and was intercepted by my favorite lifeguard, she was a senior in high school and looked like she was straight out of the swimsuit edition of Sports Illustrated. "Can you go get us ice cream?" She said. "We'll buy you and your buddy some too" "Yep" I said. "It won't make your girlfriends jealous will it?" she said with a smirk. "What? No! they aint our girlfriends" I squeeked. She wanted a chocolate sundae with extra cherries on top. We walked over to the ice cream shop and ordered their ice cream. We felt pretty cool coming back with arm loads of malts and shakes for the lifeguards, I'm sure we looked like little wet, love struck puppies. I'd already forgotten about Holly and her friends. We spent the rest of the afternoon playing catch with a football, "Beebus, Beebus," Buford would call out. I'd run the route and exaggerate my moves like someone was actually trying to tackle me. I'd dodge my way past the big cottonwood tree that acted as the goaline, "touchdown" I bragged jogging backwards with my hands up in the air.

Chapter 12

COUNTY FAIR

It's county fair time! We were staying in the fort that night so we thought it'd be fun to go to the figure 8 race and then back to the fort, it wasn't that far of a walk. "Let's go!" said Buford, "I want to play the cranes". The county fair had rides like the sizzler, ferris wheel, and a bunch of other rides that would spin you silly. We decided to ride the sizzler and puked after getting spun around like a windmill , a whole blue snow cone gone, what a waste, it took me a half an hour to be able to walk straight again.

Buford won a skull belt buckle out of the crane game, I don't think he really wanted it, he just wanted to win. The problem with him playing so many crane games is that he spent all his money on the game and didn't have any left to get into the races. "You dummy!" I said, "how are we going to get in now?" The fairgrounds were very familiar to us, we'd ride our bikes down through there all the time and we'd ride around the figure 8 track like we were racing. "Gentlemen, start your engines!" You would have thought we were at the Daytona 500 the way everyone was cheering and the revving of the engines. All for a bunch of beat up old cars that were about to run around a track flinging mud everywhere. It was the best when they smashed in the middle, they didn't want to do that but that was the best part. "I have an idea, let's sneak in" Buford said. It was risky, the whole town was there and if we got caught, everyone was going to see. "Come on you wussy!" he taunted. I guess I could have paid and let him sneak in by himself but that's not how we operated. We found a part of the wood fence that was broke and before you knew it we were under the bleachers. Just as we started to laugh about our apparent success a security guard yelled, "Hey, you kids, get back up to your seats." We looked at him, looked at each other and took off to the top side of the bleachers.

Chapter 13

EXPANSION

"We need a bathroom in here" I said. "Wait, what do mean? You're not going to poop in here are you? Buford asks. "No butthead, lets dig a deep hole over here and we can just pee in it and cover it up with a board, that way we don't have to go outside" I said. And with that the tower expansion started. The tower was to be 3 stories and would shoot up over our existing structure. We dug a tunnel out of our living room and into the bathroom. From there you went up a ladder to another room and above that was the lookout. It was pretty high up and we could see all around the neighborhood. With this additional construction we counted 9 rooms, it had become the talk of the town.

We'd always see adults driving by real slow looking at the massive wood structure that had no apparent design, yet it had a "swiss family robinson" look about it. It certainly made others jealous. With that jealousy, some decided to turn to destruction. One night, the guys we called the grits decided to break in and try to destroy the place. They had tried to scare us at night once before when we were sleeping over. We're pretty sure it was them because they had a tree house just up the tree line. They hung out there and would sneak down by ours and spy on us and make weird noises. I was the first one to see the damage and was as mad as a kid could be. When you work so hard for something and someone tries to take it away or ruin it, it's a bad feeling. It happens a lot in life but when you're a kid, its tough. They did some damage with spray paint and stole some things but really didn't impact the integrity of our creation and within a couple days it was all back to normal. We knew who they were but didn't start a war, we just watched over the place more and made the locks stronger, no way they could get in again.

Chapter 14

THE FLOOD

Summer was coming to an end and we were going to be 7th graders so the fort thing wasn't probably going to be cool for much longer. No one made fun of us or anything like that but we were going to have football and chorus practice and homework, there just wasn't going to be enough time to hang out there anymore. The best part about it was building it, we had more fun during the construction than just sitting inside of it. We decided that we could still do sleepovers in it and planned on it Friday night after the football game. My Dad stopped down and came inside before we left for the game. He was partially shocked at the look of the interior with the girly posters, knickknacks and other fort stuff but issued a fateful warning: "You guys are going to have to swim out of here tonight." It was cold that night and it had already started to rain.

At the game some of the cheerleaders were our lifeguard friends. "Here we go Spartans here we go" they cheered. The football game was secondary. We went mainly to see what girls were going to be there. We'd grown up a lot that summer, girls were starting to be cool.

 We didn't stay long at the game and headed to our warm and dry fort. We'd packed everything in earlier and all was well and dry as we knew it would be, that waterbed roof was working wonders. Little did we know there was a pool of rain forming outside our walls and little by little drips were dancing down the carpet of the couch. We were looking at our baseball cards and Buford decided to pry a little piece of carpet back from the wall. That's all it took, it was like a dam had burst.

We thought we could stop it but more cracks started leaking, water was literally coming through the walls. We had built the fort in a ditch which ended up being serious design flaw. It hadn't rained like that all summer and we were an island in the middle of a river about to go under. I grabbed what I could and headed out through the hole we made for the expansion for the tower, Buford wasn't far behind even though he decided to dive back through to save his precious George Brett. A minute before we had our prized baseball cards out and were thinking about a trade, the next minute it was chaos. He never found his George Brett card. It had been buried in 6 inches of mud that had now covered our living room and turned our tornado room into a sinkhole. We lost more than that in that 5 minute span, we had lost the fort. It wasn't coming back from this one and I think we both knew it that night as we shivered in the dim light of our flashlights.

Chapter 15

GROWING UP

We eventually tore the fort down after the carpet got all stinky from the rain and the mud that couldn't be cleaned out. The following summer we built a one room tree house. It was 10 feet off the ground and took our construction skills to a higher level. It wasn't the same as the old fort. I'd sit in there as the tree house would sway with the trees in the wind and look out the window at the old site. Just a few boards left scattered around and a partial footprint of the fort. It was ok, things change and nothing stays the same forever. I can still hear the hammers pounding, most would hit the nail, occasionally you'd hear the dead thump of the hammer hitting the wood. Each of us calling each other goofy names when we'd do something stupid. Not even time can take those memories away.

Chapter 16

GOOD TIMES

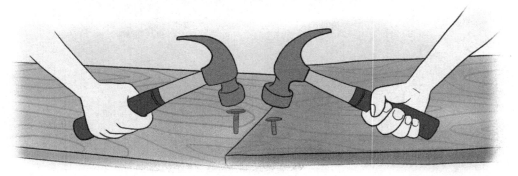

We had the greatest summer ever back in 1982. The fort was a part of us and we were a part of it. We knew everything about it, every little nook and cranny and it provided a canvas that 2 kids and 2 hammers turned into an epic masterpiece. Not only in wood but in a lifetime memory.

I went back to the fort site 20 years later, hoping to see if there were any remnants of what we had built. There were just a couple of old boards hanging on to a tree by rusty nails, the ground was covered in vegetation, no evidence that we were ever there. The trees had overgrown the area and it looked like a jungle now. I could still picture how it looked in my mind and set it back right in its old spot. I listened to the breeze in the trees and thought I heard our theme song quietly playing. Just my imagination taking me back to those good times.

Made in the USA
Monee, IL
06 January 2020

19951007R00031